BRIGHTWORD

Books by Kimberly Burwick

Custody of the Eyes
Brightword

BRIGHTWORD

Kimberly Burwick

Carnegie Mellon University Press
Pittsburgh 2019

Acknowledgments

My grateful acknowledgment to the following journals where versions of these poems have appeared:

Connotation Press: "[Surf clams vanishingly normal as some]," "[Do not rescue the total brightness]," "[The earth warms to earth's blue-crab dark]" *decomP magazinE*: "[Snow-wound, this means he has gone]," "[Never my own branches—aspen, a fraction]," "[White friction, snow more specific]" *North American Review*: "[Should we come to cover our son's aortic root]," "[Circumambulate the Sabbath, silent-leaning]" *Talking River*: "[Cold enfolding now, alder, tulip-holder]," "[On the rough edges of blue noise, crickets wing]," "[I closed my eyes—he could live a scarlet]" (appeared as "[Agreeing in solemn fiction the meadowlarks]"), "[Blue heron, that feathered tempest—]" (appeared as "[Passenger Pigeon, that feathered tempest]")

Special thanks to Rebecca Gayle Howell for her remarkable guidance in editing this collection. To Connie Amoroso, Cynthia Lamb and Gerald Costanzo for believing in this book. To Nnenna Okore for her stunning cover art. And to Katie Ford and Kaveh Akbar for their endorsements of these poems.

And especially to Kevin, always.

Cover art by Nnenna Okore. *Body Language*; Cheesecloth, burlap, jute strings, dye, and wire; 72" x 96" x 25"; 2015.

Book design by Connie Amoroso and Bernice Yu

Library of Congress Control Number 2019949336
ISBN 978-0-88748-651-7

10   9   8   7   6   5   4   3   2   1

For my son, Levi Goodan, who taught me how to see these poems, and whose observations are woven throughout.

Contents

I. Cardiac

II. Sensorium

III. Benthic

Near, in the aorta's arch,
in bright blood:
the brightword.

—Paul Celan

Wherever there is number, there is beauty.

—Proclus

I. CARDIAC

When my son's ascending aorta doubles
I map the earth that rushes on,

ask the cardiologist to calculate the curve
and value of everything chestward, brightward

beyond the pitching seeds of lilies
and lilacs as they make calm

and flesh the same green force—
the boy in symmetry and balance and dirt

his minuscule frame dense as honey
under the influence of gravity

Negative two degrees, I'm torn if his soul
will fall back, he says, *wind has no color*

and he's right—no matter here in Idaho
or the Cape's lone blue arm, the clouded health

of sky can always hesitate, grow amber,
build vapor; he raises winding ribbons

of kite and I cannot be sure
if I am near those regions where sunlight

is blocked or in the expansive layers
of motherhood full of dark, congenital math

Green unowned awe, *we are the gathers*
of mint, he says, hair of the quiver-quiet deer,

the elemental muscle of Idaho land,
damp disappearing finch with leap and doubt—

under water I remember water is also a woodland
slow in underslung balance, he watches a click beetle

and wonders if the full moon is young or claimed
or old, he wants it not because it's far

but because its shadow is a body of thistles
he cannot smell or prove or sweep

Cold enfolding now: alder, tulip-holder,
peal-call of the eagle—I know I said

you could cry; you sobbed,
your language sky-locked in steaming snow,

damp undamped, all in the burn pile

but meadowlarks, though if we suck
the blear of hymns and earthquake

the great sedum veins, what
scattering bright will have at us?

I closed my eyes—he could live a scarlet
tanager's life or keep the wound

nested for years, the boy says, *I feel the earth
chose me to be its friend,* as if moss was the last

tongue of scripture and scripture
was closer to aster holy, holy, holy—

I wanted to make sure there was both
earth and heaven, sedum and stonecrop;

mother and boy and the sheer
trigonometry of sun fresh from its rise

Rain holding down the buffaloberries,
not my wilds, mothers of weightless twist,

unbranched and branched paintbrush,
evenly chance and soured fruits unchurched

in the ordinary Palouse wind—
how we serve each interval's point,

serious about its florid farness; my boy collects
lava stones, knows a legend of the Palus tribe,

fears the rock that is Beaver's heart
left by the mouth of the river

Hold of algebra in this hawthorn gush of sun,
its science stuck in what's hung to dry:

the mint, the sedum and flutter that was
in the world, now this drifting grace of you

crushing winged ants—What kind of *we* must
we become? Neither creation nor the forking

habit of roots want an answer; *the earth is
eating breakfast*, you say, the way blood

threads the aortic arch with an eddy
of morning glories and buttercups

Ivy, calamint, the female
pine-using, cherry-using rain:

as if pollen could be divided into past
and future, the kind of growing

that sorts theology from stark
weather—in his ultrasound

the fine honeycomb formation,
lattice of cloud upon cloud

with smaller ripples in shadow

Into the discussion: his disease, then rabbits
to affirm the mayweed, even the golden ratio

of pinecones can suffer a silent dissection,
how the peace and choke of dust are proved

by these quilted acres of topsoil, so tender the boy
like quail this pure they've come

only for water, O' Lord afterward—the sun rotund
in smoke and I love as if lengthened

by blue elder and aster, fierce rags
of wind when I want to go forward

Blue heron, that feathered tempest—
earth come to life, earth come to life

the boy breathes into the huckleberry mind
of curtained lilacs, tangles of chokecherry;

I mark the center of his chest
with pollen, listen to the sounds

of S1 and S2 like the turbulence
and snap of doves,

a harmony in the convection
and inbreathing of grace

On the rough edges of blue noise, crickets wing
our blunt crossing, crowns of them crust

the wheat, they tilt and mood our ramble
until we stop at the buried boundless field,

see a bird minding her young, the desperate
lucid end of any day, this diameter

of nest large and simple to fill
with scar, and there is more—warm current

of each octave, the great palace of summer
after, and before, and after

Nothing yet enters our eyes as answers:
the clean speed of garden hose surging

across seal lavender, yellow-jacketed
in sepia-arc, the sun somehow crossing

a natural barrier toward a calculus only
mastered when we pass our hearts

along to the great tour of wind, the same animal
organ you dirt and drag, wedge and wash—

and the song, the song is so far back
in our throats we become old as born

Tetralogy of daybreak
the burning of our margins—

A workshop of meadowlarks
will float and land fir

and the essence of fir in drought,
and I—a loud crash

of woman—run the boy
through cattails and grains

with enough life to suggest
he may live

II. SENSORIUM

White friction, snow more specific
than snow or blue icicles

bedimmed and direct—
I want everything to darling you

this way: the flutter of quail
beneath nightbirds, the blooming beds

of hoarfrost growing equally
from God and my own disturbed

dawn, I want you never stained
with aortic flood, I want and wait to want

Never my own branches—aspen, a fraction
of bright cage in the yard of limb-gold

roots, crude reach of etching sun
underslung by the slightest

idea of green—the boy is everything, is vivid
in place, embedded ghost of arm-wide turns

of earth, as it is lived, as we are lived, the great
good-hearted magnitude of geese coming

ever finer in the frozen signs of clouds
flushed and sudden and engaged in shroud

Snow-wound, this means he has gone
beyond his past into the real names

for boyhood as though it were a condition
of storage in a world of drift, him

not yet brought down by the compost
of love—call the clouds we cloud-spot

dolphin, narwhal, polar cub—

claim the curve of earth is coming
straight down if we forget to be grateful

Another way I held up my soul in the racket,
the crows turned white, whiteness

was the way in, and you, you—
how much time passes is measured

in the great pressure of hanging fruit,
even lilac is a torch, and later when I fumble

in amber, the frost is infinite, is anchor
and linger, is the child who clears

his ashy throat and wants water, wants to
lunge and bridge, wants a definition

Bring the woman who irons her own land, lifting
pine needles and pitch needles, living and listing

the eye movement of robins, she must be ashamed
to err, to believe in the short reward of evergreen birds,

in the purple filter of small veins, aortic root and
its variables—new snow weighs as much as a breath

in line for another breath, or burnt stinkbugs
peeled from firewood and we slide them across the floor

and we race them in their deadness, and we ask them
to make the same noise as the musical suck of dust

Your great artery has no metaphor, will not dissolve
into middle clouds, the sudden cirrus fallstreaks,

you hold copper ice chunks on the comma
of our snowbank, the wind at wind speed, such vertebrae

in the tangled water—organs, cell parts, the definite
and indefinite integers so awkward in their charm and function,

the moan doesn't only darken it weeps dark lilacs, it ferries
a line collapsing in joy—

that you can make a castle, that rocks fall
into the whole of elements

Lavender—a woolheart, a wildeat, all soil
in one pure word—as in: being weaned,

as in: the milk-of-the-dead is the dead,
as with cows, mothers, stages of wheat:

seedling, tillering, boot-swollen
before early milk, early dough,

losing green color, the brightwall
of bastard veins in a brassy wind,

you see a deer and say, *it's a she*
I know how a girl deer ruins the apples

Russian sage, elk thistle, yarrow and pulse rate—
I see why thunder eggs did

what they did in lava flow, I have to hold first
October snow like it is utterly aflame,

a knotted maturation of brightsmoke, breaksoul—
I have to bend for each blast of rain

bringing it to behave as host and ice, red
is only for you the beckoning, the earth-hair

you were melting before school, using a wet
stick, trying to name the end of numbers

Hyacinths choose to be planted an inch deeper
for the sun will overthrow any purpose;

any name you give him
he will be the brightbearer of the bluntbulbs

the love and advance of it all, heartroot
in centimeters, mother of syllables,

how close and unbridgeable the haunting
of your breath ceasing—

goldenrod, goldenrod, sweet flag

Where a body is depends on what you said
about *the moon having nothing but path*—

I have a boy who loves everything alive,
who stills the herons and seeds the herons,

like the moment you smelled land
turning earthy overnight, the wrong

blank power of dirt shy of dust, the flies,
the dandelions you blow on

hearing breath come back as pluck

Early tests: the growing zones
of goji berries, maple in the minor arc

of acreage; I am alert to the pause
in every running game, his range for now

almost a normal artery; wicked to imagine
the teen years like buffaloberries waxy and wild;

the doctor says there is certain death
in dissection, and so I will camp

at the foot of my boy—
alive, alive, alive

Sound records its breastbone source,
kettle ponds, quartz and talc—

a bright-hymn so brushcleared
this is all I will do with my life,

nothing slow or solved
or equal to this motherhood;

you say, *the beautiful are inside stone*
and they come together to make more stone—

there are hundreds
of starting points: sparrow,

sparrow, monarchs—
it isn't hard to be alive

Say, *atmosphere*—be given
at least a model of saffron finch,

the great math of its molt
all slowed and rain,

the pattern and smokiness
of you sleeping as guest in this world,

like the solemn muscle of lilacs
laid out for vespers—

we live by numbers, the standard
deviation always written in violet-blue

Your condition—I limit myself to the terror

of quail almost indentured
to harmony, the grind of sunrise

like an abrupt return to the steadiness
of size, layout what is light and which artery

is Lord, so large—use this winter to still
all winters, geometrically we are flushed

and sudden and nothing but acres

All the mathematical warblers, moths recasting
the same course of language

Our cardiologist phrases

clamp the aorta though I prefer blue lightning,
thundering quail, spectre of the Brocken—

From the Euclidian world, I see you
playing archer toward the pitch clusters,

They send resin to flood the wound, Momma—
Did you know that? The tree makes a scab

III. BENTHIC

The green has gone to the green curves
of Cape water

Thus, we are a yard full of wheatbirds—

Quilt birdlime, quilt unbelted rain,
anything I can smell and gland

and ounce into hermit-lush, become shagbark
and little leaf, become one of many breathing

and after, when we hold our great seeds,
nothing is calm but ocean

Toward rip current the boy loads
his spirit, ties crabs to rakes,

sails bones and snails toward Spain
in rubber boots and rash guard

running left and worming where earth
will allow; it is a different dare

when he taunts the sea to last,
rooted in its benthic hum—

on his knees he tells me who
and what has left the world

Mathematician, what I need now
is a theta function for a mint-fibered heart—

In dark the Mobius wind turns into itself
because it must, because fire cherry and choke-

cherry between us are more tender infinites
than Aspen, a spill of lilacs is devoted in the end

to no peal or sound or dust—

And if, around some closed loop should
you take our apple mint, breath weaker

than yarrow, my brackets will be written as dirt
plus dogwood plus fretful ash

I'm leading you now
through the streets of Boston

back from the cardiologist, toys are dim angels
letting the autumn out of their excellent sounds,

twelve robins coming your way
in the evening, in the evening—

it's not cheating to let your pulse
into the odd trinity

of sumac, hickory, elm

What happened to the environment in his pink
mind was fat blooming cables of algebra,

the mineral grains betraying and saving
the earth, the way the beating heart

never fruits the air until it is held and doctored
with the soul-content of sparrows—

Throughout the night, the beach's plumage
was just the beginning, we spoke of

what not to do near hermit crab scraps
like the end behavior of the horizon

My boy will live another year, we'll measure
the scrimshaw

inside his chest, wash sand from razor clams—

The ocean is formed and we become salt grass,
spike rush, the benthic zone

red in its starchy tenor of depth;

the forecast for June

is still aortic—recite, I am mother of the soft sediment

it's only water, I am only the mother

We strain for the lullaby but it's bright
red in our wash of throats,

frogs everywhere at home, but here
we are ocean-faced

with pontoon cuts, light brushwood, the bay

exquisite in its guiding and guesswork—
What fantasy of water is not static?

Close up the jetty is smashed, wind in the arms

of our boy purring to wind-maker

The air is actually blowing
through them, dead or not

but what does it mean, the skeleton of a fish,
the fish's pale stripes before mackerel clouds,

the atmosphere said to be stable
at the gates of a more sedate love?

It's easy to forget birds gliding
the wind shear,

the sequence that will rush us
with no bodies for glory

Surf clams vanishingly normal as some
burdened pulsing light

that separates dusk from bass,
chicory from buoyancy, the area

underneath a curve of peridot becomes
periwinkle—

we call for geese like geese,

their warm, travelled route makes arcs
like bluefish falling out of the sky,

their scales confetti us, our eyes and gaze

Do not rescue the total brightness
of the next turnings

of tide, osprey not a word but a rising;
revolving claim that water

is helpless as water, you stab the hermit
shell with a clamming rake, insects just so

in the light, unto that hatch
the earth is headed unheeded

though we tell the ocean birds
the colors we've found in sand

Forswear the ferry and what's left is whale
upon whale, so many humpbacks says the guy

who rents our dock, pods in cold
honey, small princes spouting the sun, the sun—

In Newfoundland when scientists plastinated
a 400-pound blue whale heart, it took seven people

eight hours to wrap it; wake our boy's
own organ and it will sputter to taste itself,

it will cut us into two camps: the saints we clock
or the dams we call cherry stones

Brightword, Brightward—bold
melting hours, can we drift?

Whales each day, the boy with me
cutting tides with a splintered stick,

clams come back, our sleeves rolled wet,
the noise of us as mother-son, as birds

on a bridge, terns that village such jetties
with crying and belonging and light-rose

trails of nautical dusk, Brightword,
Brightward—I want to go with you

Circumambulate the Sabbath, silent-leaning
the unfolded geese, one of them hideously

free of meaning, one stained over
her gosling, dented upon the blue waters

entirely defined by sand unlike Galileo
who could not imagine magnitudes

might differ in size; the whale keeps
to his warm blood as I to my boney son,

it's blistering to think of disobeying
ourselves, doing nothing but wading tides

The continent of elements
is a continent of love,

equations even souls
couldn't block,

I think nature can hear us,
likes to hear

what we say, I set a little fire
I set a little soul out

for earth,
let me hunt the juniper burn

to give the continent
love, the delicate wake

we were at birth, *the water rises*
until someone nice comes along

and fills the sky
with cardiac dust

The earth warms to earth's blue-crab dark
then comes the soul with gull breath,

water dressing up the sand
with weather, the boy is built of cloud-melt

and tiny settlements of glory—
hair, body, nails—sun alone

far above, cluttered with scent, the whole
poisoned sea-rhythm still sure enough

to go on toward cut muscle and cod

Should we come to cover our son's aortic root
with saline particle and wreck

there will be no roar, days having swept
snow from hairline and the neck of little blue

gloves, the quail, the number of sheep, deep earth
he has rested and questioned

the physics of afterworlds, foxes,
anchor-points of sun; the benthic in me

is peat-meadow, cedar-cut, entrance
and wind, I want this closed cove

to form a beach